THE LIGHTNING FIELD

Carol Moldaw

THE LIGHTNING FIELD

Carol Moldaw

Oberlin College Press

http://www.oberlin.edu/~ocpress

Publication of this book was supported in part by a grant from the Ohio Arts Council.

Ohio Arts Council
A STATE AGENCY
THAT SUPPORTS PUBLIC
PROGRAMS IN THE ARTS

Library of Congress Cataloging-in-Publication Data

Moldaw, Carol.
        The Lightning Field / Carol Moldaw.
        (The FIELD Poetry Series v. 14)
        I. Title.   II. Series.

LC: 2003101739
ISBN: 0-932440-94-0 (pbk.)

for Arthur

Acknowledgments

Grateful acknowledgment is made to the editors of the following publications in which these poems, sometimes in earlier versions, previously appeared:

AGNI: "The Lightning Field," section 1
Anthology of New Mexico Poets, 1960-2000: "Anastylosis"
The Antioch Review: "Insomnia"
Blue Mesa Review: "The Lightning Field," section 11
The Blue Moon Review: "Lou Reed in Istanbul," "Pelagos"
Chicago Review: "The Lightning Field," sections 5, 8, 14, and 15
Colorado Review: "Studies in Pen and Ink," sections 1 and 4; "The Lightning Field," section 4
Conjunctions: "Festina Lente"
Denver Quarterly: "Studies in Pen and Ink," sections 2, 3, and 6; "The Lightning Field," sections 1, 7, and 13
The Drunken Boat: "Studies in Pen and Ink"; "The Lightning Field"
FIELD: "Appraisal," "Geese," "Wind above the Weather"
First Intensity: "Anastylosis"
Forward: "Timetable for Birds"
Manoa: "The Lightning Field," sections 6, 9, and 10
The New Republic: "Conduit"
The Paris Review: "The Lightning Field," sections 3 and 16
Parnassus: "Report"
Pushcart Prize XXVII: Best of the Small Presses: "The Lightning Field," sections 5, 8, 14, and 15
The Threepenny Review: "Studies in Pen and Ink," section 5
Volt: "The Lightning Field," section 12
Web Conjunctions: "The Lightning Field," section 5

My admiration as well as my thanks go to my editor, Martha Collins, and to all of my editors at Oberlin: Pamela Alexander, David Walker, and David Young.

Contents

Studies in Pen and Ink

1.
A cigarette tucked at a rakish angle
behind a donkey driver's ear,

a gold coin in the ear's whorl;
a man and a woman behind him

in his cart, while a woman in a silk chemise
stands to adjust her garter and black stocking,

one foot up on the nearest wheel,
a man's disjointed arm jutting between her legs,

in his fist a rock, aimed at a rottweiler.
"Krishna" in parenthesis—the driver's name.

2.
Taped to a self-portrait:
a news clipping, an AP photo
of four Croatian soldiers mugging
for the camera, in what was then
Tomislavgrad, Yugoslavia.
The artist looks like herself,
and one of the soldiers looks
like the artist, which must be why
she thought to make the sketch.

Both women's waists are cinched
over bulky camouflage jackets; each
has one foot off the ground,
as if leaping; both smile, dimpled,
exuberant; a pistol handle sticks out
of each one's side pant pocket;
each raises two fingers in a V,
but only the real soldier
has nail polish visible on her thumb.

3.
Bite marks on a bent foreknuckle.
Fingers spread to press flat

a poem's crumpled tear sheet.
Wrists at the center of a pinwheel.

Going clockwise, the crosshatched
overlapping hands: cupped,

relaxed, grasping, clenched,
and then a knotted rheumatoid claw.

Index and middle fingers raised
in a V; repeated once, turned

sideways, a pair of scissors
snipping, snipping away at the page.

4.
The man and the woman
whose breast he cups from behind
exist on the same plane,

while the sprawling man
whose hand clutches for her thigh,
and the woman who leans over

the edge of the bed, the man
pursing his lips, and the one
kneeling to pray, are drawn

at diagonals and the contact
they make is wayward, tangential.
Her eyes are closed. Her hands

are bound. Her hands are
half-erased. She has more arms
than Vishnu. Arching one

behind her, she encircles
her lover's head, and pressing
the base of his skull,

presses his mouth to her neck.
Hands crumple the bedsheets,
open like a lotus. One covers

the hand at her breast, one's flat
at her side. One's crooked
at the elbow, suppressing a yawn.

5.
The strawberry da Vinci drew in cross-section
on one side of a notebook page bleeds through

to cushion a fetus floating on the back.
By now, the ink has browned, the paper's cracked,

dimly lit, encased upright and displayed
in glass for us to circle, case after case

of notebook pages we pause before and pass
in accelerating knots and curlicues—

*the coition of a hemi-sected man
and woman* no more absurd or accurate

than a flying machine. A tube from the testicles,
the seat of ardor, leads straight to the heart.

Once, in a videotape of surgery,
I saw fimbria wafting in the body's fluid

like seaweed under water. The ovaries looked
like sponge or coral. Here, the woman's heart's

a dial. I hear my own timer ticking,
ticking fast, the parts dissected, tagged,

and reassembled, but never yet disarmed.
Or detonated. Here, here's the blueprint,

recto and verso, marked up in mirror script.
The deeper I delve, the more I feel objective.

Pushed by the crowd, we rush through in under an hour:
a living page, one of the studies on water.

6.
Landscape with a corn snake
sunning itself on a husked branch
of a dead tree. Afternoon shade
gloves a left hand. The waterfall's

diaphanous shawl's a yashmak,
leaves only the eyes unveiled—
the third eye, like a horse's blaze
on the stone forehead. Hoofprints

brand the wet grass; the pool's
scattershot with catkins and leaves.
Rock moss oozes between my toes
as I wade in, testing the water,

the watermark, the ink, the line,
the line of argument, the pen.
—And in my hair, a myriad
of nests, one for every bird.

Festina Lente

Rake marks on gravel.
Flecks of straw in adobe.

Four and a half feet down,
a blue-glass flask flaking mica,

charred wood, a layer of ash,
a humerus, if not animal,

then human. What looks
like the slatted side of a crate,

the backhoe driver says
is an old well shaft.

Mounds of displaced dirt,
dug up for new leach lines,

rise higher than the walls.
All we know of the pueblo

is that they burned trash here,
in our courtyard; spoke Tewa;

and dispersed—were driven out—
to Santa Clara, to Hopi.

Did the same ditch irrigate
their beans as our flowering plums?

And where we sleep, is that
where their turkeys flocked?

The man who built this house,
scavenging bridge ties for beams,

died in the courtyard,
his sickbed facing sunrise.

His wife's "stitcheries"
still cover some windows.

When we reburied the humerus
under a cottonwood, with incense

and a patchwork prayer,
we were only putting it back,

festina lente, into the mix
of sieved dirt, sand, and straw.

Appraisal

Five glass hearts to a hoop.
Chinese coins knotted onto brown silk.
Two sterling silver girls skipping gold wire ropes.

Three emerald beryl beads.
A waterfall of three freshwater pearls.

Angel skin coral cabochons.
Milligrain-edged salmon-colored coral briolettes.

Filligreed dangles.
French screwbacks.

A pair of bezel-set mine-cut diamonds, hinge-hooked.

Her mother's mabé pearls.
Her father's gold-flecked agate eyes.
Sapphires snipped out of a coat's silk lining.

Emerald-cut glass.
A cracked turquoise heart.

Teardrop pearls, off-round to the eye.
One of the silver girls, dew-tarnished.

His angel-skin skin.
Her slippery cabochon.

Lou Reed in Istanbul

In the poem I had in mind
one blue-tiled stanza
containing a striped divan
and a single cut tulip
ends at a latticed window

behind whose fretwork
an entire regiment
of red-turbaned tulips
is posted, standing guard
with drawn daggers.

Steam obscured one stanza,
making its marble sweat,
veiling its women's naked
boredom with languor,
their faint mustachios

with clove-scented dew
(dew that dissolves
on the tongue like sugar
but tastes bitter-briny,
indigestible as tears).

A sinuous line of incense
led to an inner courtyard
where someone crouched
over a brass brazier, fanned
wisps of musky smoke

up the bellows of her skirt.
Hearing the click-clack
of my heels on the cobble
she turned to appraise me,
quickly got back to work.

That mother-of-pearl
intarsiate poem, poem
of the narrow-necked vase,
the bejeweled mirror,
of pumice and water pipes

and plush labyrinthian
women who glide up
from the foot of the bed,
who hide their emotions
even from the moon—

Lou Reed shanghaied
that poem, he runs
its arched passageways
despotic as a eunuch,
slouches on its pillows,

the sheer-stockinged
corseleted cross-dresser
on *Transformer*'s cover,
where, in Bilbao at 17,
listening to "Vicious,"

to "Satellite of Love,"
in a Spanish boy's bed
a year before Franco
finally died, high
on codeine cough syrup,

I first saw him, his prick
in the facing photo
a concealed nightstick.
Now, listening to his
roughed-up deadpan

under a domed moon
just up the Bosphorus
from Topkapi's seraglio,
watching some starlings
swoop toward the stage

to flit in the lights,
I remember how it felt,
the blood rush—*swoop,
swoop, oh baby, rock,
rock*—of being set loose.

Insomnia

I feel *something*
        —I'm not sure what—
                            it's too many layers down
       to name
               clitoral itch
                      the size of a flea bite
     chocolate cyst
          pea gravel   occluded bruise

between me and sleep
               a ditch too big . . .
      leaping would wake me

          for each nub in the coarse cotton sheets
               the prickle of leg-hair against my thigh
     an adjustment
              a re-arrangement

between waking and sleep:
          the day's footage

   a controlled burn gone wild
            smoke plumes carried over the canyons
        the rotating arrows of an anchorman's wind-map

   a friend who every day in the markets of Laos
               ate coagulated pig's blood
      mistaking it for marinated tofu:
   by the time he admitted
                  he didn't want to live with D
     he was already fucking A

                   at the stop light
         a sleek black   unleashed lab
                        pacing the bed of a pickup
                                      clawing the molded walls

between me and sleep
                        a door jammed shut
           an untried window
                        plastic rain gutter   from which to dangle
                                                  from which to fall

         squeal of a baby raccoon   in the cattails   being torn apart
                   by dogs   my dog
                             my fingers   twisted in his collar

                   my arm   forced between the fence-wires

between waking and sleep
                                      two blossoming pear trees
           outside a squat brick building in Socorro

20

Pelagos

1.
A man takes a walk on the beach below his house,
throws a fluorescent tennis ball into the waves—

his face lighting up as he describes the intricate
simplicities of Japanese building technique,

the temple at Kiyomizu, with its healing water-
fall (and not a single nail)—tries to remember

the name of a book. He can picture the layout
of a page he wants to show us, the photograph

of scaffold, roof beam, and joists, but the title
is iced sake evaporated on the tip of his tongue.

Bending for the ball his dog retrieved from the waves
and dropped at his feet, careful to keep his head

above the bloodline of his heart, he looks up as if
to say "This is absurd," straightens, shakes off

his residue of fear, tosses the ball into the breakers.
Roof beam, tennis ball, book; sake, bloodline, wave.

He would like to go back to Kyoto someday, someday
go back to Greece. But for now, each step of the steep

crooked beach stair scaling the hill back to his house
is a whitecap requiring a surfer's obstinate strength.

In the clear sea of his sun-stricken eyes, on the swell
of his unremitting gaze, an uncertain skiff.

2.
Though I'd let it languish next to my chaise
almost two years, as soon as you died I took up

the Seferis you'd sent me, reading at first
only notes inked in your hand, marked phrases,

studying ruefully the locked diary of words
written out in your fluent-looking Greek:

every dog-ear, the signature of unglued pages,
the smudged binding, your name on the flyleaf,

even the Hellenic Bookservice label at first
talismanic as the sea, the harbor, the pines.

> *friend who left for the island of pine-trees*
> *friend who left for the island of plane-trees*
> *friend who left for the open sea*

All week I've been searching for my poem,
a handful of lines, how could I lose them?

Could a copy still be folded in thirds
and tucked inside the collected cummings

I snuck into an open box of your books?
"Greek Dancer" I think I called it . . .

did you *ever* come across it? For years,
when you were alive but more vanished

from my life than now, I let myself regret
only the velvet jacket left in your pickup.

the life they gave us to live, we lived

From the house you built, and the meadow
where a yellow dog snuffles in tall grass,

you can see your wife and twin tow-headed sons
looking out over the cliffs to the kelp beds

where your ashes were launched from your kayak
and strewn like phosphorus on the pulsing skin

of the sea. When we meet now, in the uncertain
pelagos of dreams, it is and is not as before,

when I could slip a poem like this into a book
and eventually, eventually, you would find it.

for Hank Palmieri

Conduit

Because the branches of the tall trees surrounding us
are winter bare, the moon has been able to project
its luminance more than usual these past few nights.
I went to bed thinking about the Pashtun word
that translates as "man-with-no-penis" and means
"man-who-doesn't-beat-his-wife," but woke up
thinking about a writer I used to know, a woman
whose re-marriage was featured in the Sunday *Times*.
In our courtyard, above the spindle-tip branches,
the moon looked sublime, unfazed by footprints
and flags, the cost of reflecting back to us our secrets
from the one side of its surface ever available
to be read into. Once, on a transatlantic red-eye,
eye level with the moon, I stayed awake all night
leveling with myself, my life stripped clean
under the discipline of her indifferent gaze.
—O Moon, what I want back now is not my naïveté
but my nerve, through which your implacable waves ran.

The Lightning Field

1.

Four hundred equidistant stainless steel poles,
twenty-five by sixteen, gird and grid the mile-long
kilometer-wide field that was once a plain.
Like polished spears, with solid tapered tips,
they rise over twenty feet. Sounding the air,
attuned to the light's least vibrato,
between dawn and dusk they all but disappear.
It was the hope of lightning drew us here,
and for an hour or so there *is* lightning—
violet strikes, frequent, sharp, and silent
above the mountains ringing the plain
but the poles do not require lightning, they
are aggregate enough. Would we have walked
so casually into the scrub and desert plain
without the reassurance of these metes
and bounds? Past the first gulch, before we reach
the corner pole, the cabin drops below
our line of sight. Quickly, characterize
and distinguish the mountains to the west from the range
to the east. The north. The south. *But we could rely
on the sun,* you say before I've had a chance
to get my bearings, your profile still so new,
studying not the mountains, but the cloud-
lit sky. Leaving the perimeter, we work
our way in, zigzagging from pole to pole.

2.
Like an opti-visored basket restorer
interlacing hidden stitches of monocord
to repair a bell-shaped Pomo burden basket,
or like the spider who seemed to be asleep
at the center of a shimmering orb web
that hung by one filament to the bottom knob
of the bronze lantern left of my front door,
until my foot grazed the lower guy wire
and the web collapsed on itself like a string bag,
like a convoluted sentence lacking syntax—
the brain surgeon left signs of his handiwork:
minuscule clips on four arterial walls
and a neatly sutured horseshoe of a scar.
At first, the spider scaled the topmost thread,
retreating to the safety of the lantern,
not so unlike, to the bleeding basket restorer,
the teetering safety of an ambulance
when, last fall, in the middle of the night,
brushing his teeth after a late video
he seized up and fell to the saltillo tile.
Next time I thought to look, the spider, true
to her nature, had rebuilt the radial web.
Just so, they say, will neurons compensate
when some are severed—firing new circuits
across the brain's electrochemical paths.

3.
Although the land itself is rolling and pitted,
the pole-tips form a horizontal plane
flat enough to support a sheet of glass.
Walking among them, you don't notice
the poles' lengths vary by over seven feet—
they look identical; what is disarming
is the languor-inducing rhythm of their recurrence.
They are far enough apart that as you walk
between them it is hard to keep in mind
the multi-angled interrelationships
that subtly tug at you from all directions
when you stop next to any one of them.
Or is it that walking two hundred and twenty feet
(three hundred and eleven, cutting across
the diagonal) allows you to forget?
You might be holding hands, stumbling over
the rough terrain, listening hard for crickets,
absorbed in particular by nothing,
maybe mulling over the near-homonyms
"liar" and "lyre," or talking of love, your love,
and how the breasts on Michelangelo's women
are like sacs affixed to a man's musculature,
when, mid-sentence, you are stopped short
by an innocuous-looking juncture, and forced
to scrutinize the meaning of your next step.

4.

Because, as the artist states in his sheet of facts,
"isolation is the essence of land art,"
we were dropped off with two days' worth of food,
having left our car miles behind in Quemado.
Before driving away, the caretaker pointed out
an emergency short-wave radio and assured us
she'd come back to pick us up in forty-eight hours.
Left to ourselves, it didn't take long to discover,
flush with the rough-hewn wall, a secret door,
which, when pushed, sprang open to reveal
mop, bucket, broom, Ajax, and rubber gloves
at the foot of a short set of stairs. These led
to a half attic, too small to stand upright in,
but big enough for the desk and swivel chair
I found—and on that desk, a working phone.
Triumphant as a child who's ferreted out
some slippery unadulterated truth,
I heard the dial tone and ran back down.
But neither of us had any use for my news.
Watching you build a fire in the wood stove,
I rocked in the pine rocker and while we talked
I thought about art's need for subterfuge—
how no construction's straightforward as it seems,
how even the comprehensive-seeming account
of this project's installation omits its cost.

5.

Your mind unkinks itself like carded wool
as one foot steps in front of the other, circling
the five-foot figure-eight infinity loop
painted on tarmac at the beach's edge
in Bolinas. Soon, like a Himalayan ascetic,
you've walked yourself into a waking trance,
not breaking pace for any passerby
who cuts into your path, only asking a man
to move his motorcycle when he begins
to park it where one end of the eight loops back.
You've heard that if a silkworm's cocoon is softened
with water, a continuous thread of silk
will unravel for a thousand yards, and you think
the spool a spider draws from must be endlessly
self-renewing, her many spinnerets
producing thread as her design requires.
You keep walking. With each successive loop,
you are being unwound and reconfigured,
a skein of slub silk crisscrossed between thumb
and little finger of an outstretched palm.
Weavers call this bundling a butterfly.
On your way home, a brood of Monarchs hovers
over a field of purple milkweed, roosting.
But one moment you could put your finger on?
There were no omens, only unread signs.

6.

a patch of virga/a verse paragraph
slant marks/slashing the sky/silvered in a shaft
of sunlight/pellucid virgules marking time
and pitch in a run of silent recitativo
no skittering drops/no rivulets of rhyme
shearing off the windshield/dripping from eaves
from leaves/self-contained/this sheet of rain
evaporates/is throttled/bottlenecked
in the sky's throat/never nears/never
grazes/never wets/the tantalized ground
virginal downpour/suspended mid-fall
coitus interruptus/a phone call/a second
thought/a punctured tire/a pummeled breast
no/no/no/no/no
the milk/won't come/the seed/won't plant/the womb
nulliparous/swells anyhow/the rain
falls/and does not fall/stalled/the drops
make no discernible sound/a sob/a soughing
at the wheel/to our right/never overhead
not in reach/always down the road
an etching/scraped/scraped out/scarring the sky
a series of caesuras/a fractured field
a field of splintered bones/of lines broken
into spits smaller than feet/smaller than
a fetus/embryonic/the arrested rain

7.

You could be on a roof hoisting a pipe,
soaking your blistered feet in Epsom salts,
spraying hydrangeas with a garden hose,
ordering pizza, or fiddling with the tiller,
when, before you know it, you've been zapped
by a lightning bolt's millisecond mega-volts.
You might come to curled up in a gravel pit
fifteen feet beyond where you last stood,
your portable radio melted to the spot.
Later you'll say it was like a shot of speed,
or like a bunch of ants running around
inside your body biting. You might have
entrance and exit burns, migraines, nausea,
tingling, blackouts, seizures, kidney damage,
damaged eardrums, sexual dysfunction.
Or like the woman in her son's kitchen
cutting broccoli by an open window,
being struck by lightning could provide
a cure. Though the current knocked her down,
first striking her right foot then traveling up
her leg, up the steel bar implanted when,
a year before, she'd broken her hip in a fall,
when she stood again, a moment later,
her bum leg, which, she said, dragged behind her
"like a sandbag," was completely healed.

8.

I had thought the rectangle of steel shafts
would feel imposed upon the pristine landscape,
an arbitrary post-modern conceit
spoiling the view. But once inside the matrix,
surrounded by the austere expanse, the sleek
sparsely planted forest of tempered poles
fanning out and lofting above me, I found
that the field's exactingly strict geometry
yielded not just jackrabbits, lizards,
blue-winged moths, gilia, and grasshoppers
flinging themselves against my face, but also
a sense of seemingly endless possibility.
Pacing the distance between adjacent poles,
from one vertex to the next we stopped to plot
a makeshift constellation's coordinates,
our footsteps connecting points like dashes to dots
in a child's draw-by-number book of stars.
That no pole stands at the rectangle's center
makes mathematical sense (it's not a square)
but came as a surprise. I'd been keeping count
under my breath, though the farther in we got
the more they blurred together at the far verge.
Midway between the two most central poles
was only a scuffed clod of desert scrub—
an omphalos among the obelisks.

9.

At the center of the world, a seismic hole
cut out of a jade disk inscribed with signs
delicate as a sandpiper's tracks at low tide;
a wrought iron bed in a bare room, a star
of Zion patchwork quilt; your hands, my hips;
falling asleep still joined; every trap
sprung free. Smegma, at the umbilicus,
and bitter ululations for the dead,
love's untranslatable glossolalia
welling up in my throat, tonguing my ear.
Is it a faulty O-ring causes leakage
between worlds, the mystic's watery eye,
the desert altar's perennially trickling spring?
No amount of celestial calculations
can explain that bolt from the blue, that pure
engine of divine kindness that brought us
face to face. At the center of the world,
two molted eagle feathers: one that stands
in a bud vase filled with salt, one held up
by a screw eye. Looking across the room
as caravans of clouds, slow wagon trains,
lumber across the window's quartered plains,
I want to rouse you out of your light sleep,
let you demonstrate, as the clouds drift,
how thoroughly you penetrate my world.

10.

Remember the row of *lux perpetua* candles
lining your bedroom's brick-propped plywood shelf,
each votive wrapped in waxy red-striped paper
stamped with the Virgin's upturned suffering face?
And how, hidden behind the left-hand speaker,
you had a box—no, a *carton* of condoms?
Looking knee to knee at Vermeer's "Lacemaker,"
you showed me how you saw in the loose strands
that overflow the velvet sewing box
an image of the imagination's bounty.
I said that I saw thread, a pair of hands,
a girl's head bent down in taxing concentration,
her own handworked collar framing her face.
I remember you walking backwards into your room,
drawing me with you, toward you, by both hands,
the bundle of fifty yarrow stalks I'd brought
still splayed out on the front room's floor, one stalk
still set apart to stand for the Infinite,
"beginningless beginning and endless end,"
according to the xeroxed instruction sheet.
Not then, not yet, not that first night, but later,
now, I see how liminal and charged
we were in the laced and spiky candlelight,
bending to meet the mattress on the floor,
to meet like changing lines in a full embrace—

11.
Wheelchair to walker to four-prong to cane,
to sometimes, as now, with only the support
of a leg brace, a man (who trekked Nepal
as a teen) works his way back to daydreamed
weekends of catch-and-release fly fishing,
foamy water surging around high boots
that neither leak nor slip. Circling the couch
and coffee table counterclockwise first,
then clockwise, then back, doing an about-face
every few rounds, he tells me as I sit,
my head swiveling, how with a brain injury
like his, affecting the arachnoid membrane,
the farthest points—hands as well as feet—
are last to heal. After a year and a half,
the swath of hair razored out in pre-op
has long been long enough to cover the scar,
but results from recent biofeedback testing
show spatial disorientation, and one hand
hasn't regained its grip—although, he says,
sitting back down, the true imprisonment
doesn't come from the body's limitations,
the most stubborn fucker is still the mind.
"If you look long enough at an abyss
an abyss gazes back at you." His laugh,
always warm and throaty, climbs to a roar.

12.
lucid/before the shutter shuts/ox bone
tortoise shell/veins on the back of a hand
lightning's return stroke/a calligraphic
radical/incised in ionized air
abrupt illuminant/shape-shifting glyph
revealing/not what I want/but what *is*
imprinted on the eye/a pseudomorph
ghost weave of disintegrated silk
lozenge-patterned/sawtooth twill/lodged
in the bronze axe/patina it once protected
the fiber purified/the line/distilled
like a thumbprint/secreted in beeswax
a six-week embryo/scanned/on the screen
the ultrasound/grainy as an etch-a-sketch
scanned/then bled out/without/a heartbeat
not "what I want"/but to accept/*what is*
to discern *caul*/from *cowl*/*cowl*/from *shroud*
the unborn/from the dead/grieving from grief
love/help me brush the cinder from my hair
this morning thunder woke me before dawn
patulous with desire/aching to be
part of the rain/pelting the skylight/part
of lightning's jagged latticework/but what
is rain/or lightning/to me/what could I
listening in bed/possibly be/to the rain

13.
The weekend we were at the lightning field
there was no moon. You can't see any lights
from other houses there—there are no houses
(except the caretaker's, which you can't see).
And since there are no highways and no streets—
only the private miles-long dirt road
on which the caretaker drives you in and out—
there are no street and highway lights, no cars,
and no car beams. Also, no town, glimmering
in the distance, no neon casino signs, searchlights,
or brightly lit little league baseball parks.
Once we switched off the few electric lights
inside the cabin, the only source of light
to obscure and/or obliterate the stars
was our flashlight's dim and flickering ray
which you kept trained a foot ahead of our feet,
steering us safely down the kitchen steps
and on for several yards, until the cabin
didn't impede our view of the sky. Then,
like lovers anywhere, the flashlight off,
we stood, eyes closed, and kissed, my back
against your chest, your arms around my waist,
my neck craned back, but not to look, not yet,
at the stars, shifting on their celestial poles,
like voyeurs angling for a better view.

14.
Walking back, as if an axis had gone slack,
we didn't feel that geometric pull
on where we stood and which way we proceeded;
let loose, we were free to cut across the field,
to circumvent the poles, to stop counting.
The meticulously placed prefabricated poles
had come to seem as natural as the cholla
and locoweed the wind sowed here and there.
We barely noticed them, as we wandered out,
we'd grown so used to their enigmatic presence,
and reaching the field's edge we stepped beyond it
without a thought, before we even knew.
Then, on the porch landing, we turned to look.
It must have been the angle of the sun
that made them practically invisible,
consumed by light the way an echo will
consume a sound, and silence consume an echo,
and yet in the air they reverberated still,
a soundless echo of their solid selves,
staves of a faded score—not wholly lost,
not like one of Bach's cantatas being wrapped
around the roots of a transplanted sapling,
or greased and folded up to hold a measure
of grain, the paper scarcer, of more worth
to his widow sold as paper than as song.

15.
Indelible as the potter's smudged thumbprint
on a carbon-dated thousand-year-old shard;
as the silk route traced back to a shred of silk
plaited in an Egyptian mummy's hair;
as a leaf-shaped lime burn scarring a left wrist;
as Cossack hooves heard from inside a cold oven—
while to someone else the rain brings back nights
of caged silkworms chewing on mulberry leaves,
and for me, walking the city's gridded blocks,
tears that didn't fall but never stopped
sounding inside me. Until all at once they did
stop, leaving an exquisite quiet,
and the air clear. As after a lightning storm,
when the sky's electrical balance is restored,
quintillions of electrons having swarmed
earthward, through a channel five times as hot
as the sun. As my friend described the bodiless voice
it could not have been more emphatic or distinct:
"Not one breath, not one heartbeat, is your own."
After that, he never took psilocybin again,
and began keeping his Covenant with God.
Before searching the sky for Hyakutake,
first I trained my binoculars on you.
In the desert, your eyes must be strong as stone.
But come, close them now, rest them in this dark.

16.
Seen from above, I think the lightning field
must look like a bed of nails, or garden spikes,
a force field of ambiguous auspices,
an artifact with calendric implications.
Although an aerial survey did determine
which way the field was positioned on the land,
the artist declares that an aerial view
is of no value—the experience takes place
within the field, walking among the poles,
in a small group, or alone. Set in concrete
foundations one foot down and three feet deep,
each pole—engineered to hold its own
in wind up to one hundred miles per hour
and cut to within an accuracy of one
one-hundredth of an inch to its own length—
is a single line in an abstract poem,
the surface repetition unfathomable
while meaning accrues across the full array
which never can be walked the same way twice.
I *wanted* to retrace our steps, the air
to vibrate with the same electric hum,
unseen cicadas, flashes of forked lightning,
but the terrain shifted under my feet,
and each confluence I thought I recognized
a play of light invariably transformed.

Timetable for Birds

Days I've spent brooding over this timetable—
a schedule for birds I can't identify
in Kansas City, a place I've never been.

According to it, a cedar waxwing's routine
is irregular, but a catbird can be clocked:
arrival 4:30, departure 9:25 (date unspecified).

Where the birds come from—where the birds go—
vagaries of wind—velocity—fate—how much
food (sleep) they need—are matters the timetable

doesn't address. Even what's relatively simple,
like who choreographs the interplay
of multiple flight paths across the sky,

or how twenty-three species all due to land
at 5:01 coordinate their simultaneous descents,
is beyond its scope. (What can't be answered

often goes untouched.) A few of the sightings—
of cardinal, kingbird, red-headed woodpecker,
chimney swift, goldfinch, meadowlark—

are confirmed by someone's light pencil mark.
Five out of six catalogued owls—great horned,
long-eared, barred, barn, and screech—

are residents who never leave. The short-eared owl
arrives at 10:10 (A.M.? P.M.?), departs at 3:15.
The least bittern, the short-billed marsh wren

arrive together (4:10) and stay the summer,
while the lapland longspur and arctic towhee
winter over. Some birds—the shoveler,

the blue-winged teal—were seen leaving
but no one knows what time they came;
others, like the coot, duly checked in

 (2:30) but managed to lift off undetected.
And you? Will your arrival, your crowning,
be clocked? A penciled note, a bracelet

of red thread twining your fledgling wrist?

Geese

We called them ducks, but they were geese, Canadian geese.
When they dipped their beaks into the water to nibble pond-scum
their tails tipped up, and their bodies bobbed, like buoys—
      a row of geese, a string of buoys.

For two weeks we watched them from the windows and deck
of our rented boat-house overlooking the salt-water pond.
Beyond the edge of the pond, which wasn't that far, you could see
      a rocky beach, a strip of sea.

The gestation had just begun. Swimming through moon jellies
and reeds to the middle of the pond, I liked to see how close I could get
to the placidly floating ducks, which is how I thought of the geese.
      Flotilla of ducks, armada of geese.

So as not to disrupt the delicate orchestration going on within,
I swam side stroke, gliding along the surface of the water like one
of the geese, one of the ducks, my eyes fixed on the shore.
      Idle moorings, the houses on shore.

But each time I swam in the pond, the pond reeds ribboned
and swirled over my thighs, exerting such a gently seductive suction
that I imagined them pulling me down, onto a bed of reeds—
      a sea-creature's lair, the swaying reeds.

And though we were already home by the time the bleeding began,
looking back now I can remember pushing aside what part of me knew
as I looked out the window, weighing my breasts in my hands,
      watching the geese, my breasts in my hands.

Wind above the Weather

Not through my body but through another's:
and where she went, you went; what she ate, what she felt,
enscrolled on your mesoderm; her voice, gait, nerves,
the vibration of the pond where you floated,
water lily, winter lotus, your long stem rooted
deep in her aqueous world until you swam out,
not out of my body, but out of your first mother's body,
out in a rush of her waters, out
beyond where she could keep you—.
Now, before we meet,

high above the pattern of prevailing winds,
above the baffling doldrums, the monsoons,
horse latitudes, westerlies, trade winds,
above even the jet streams that snake and loop
across the world in great meandering waves,
is a wind above the weather
drifting slightly with the earth's rotation
as it blows between us, from me to you, you to me:
first we are connected by this wind,
instrument of prayer.

Report

The articulation of my bones
a bird's, I woke not just not knowing
where or who but *what* I was:
my opened arm a wing in which she rested,
the two of us fuscous and fused
in the feathery half-dark
until that consciousness that's always
roving, testing, that's roving now,
striving to assemble an accurate report,
probed further into the feeling
and found me made of string and straw,
bits of silky floss licked together,
a nest shaped to fit her unfledged shape,
an account of ourselves I accepted
until daylight pried apart the louvers
and I discovered myself fingering
the soft stubble of her shaven hair.

Birthstone

Each morning I eat an orange
from the bagful given us
by the head of the orphanage
and still the bag is full.

Afternoons on the tour bus
you sit in my lap and sleep
or cling to my garnet necklace
biting it with all four teeth.

Out the bus's window
the bicyclists of Guangzhou
balance boxed refrigerators
and crates of live hens

above their back spokes.
Look ma, no hands
another new parent jokes
as he refocuses his lens

to catch a trio of girls
turning perfect cartwheels
before they begin to squeal
and mug for the camera.

A cluster of girls that age
and one albino boy
posed for their pictures
that day at the orphanage.

"Welcome American families"
the chalkboard read.
These are our best babies
your father overheard

someone say in Mandarin
as you were carried in
and I shot out of my seat
to take you from your "auntie"

and hold you close.
You were wearing layers
on layers of clothes
topped by bulging ovcralls

and pink appliquéd
white cotton shoes
too small for your toes
but soft and delicate.

Yours. And you *mine.*
Under close-cropped hair
your big eyes took me in
with a glint of recognition.

Then, after an exchange
of currency and gifts,
everyone stood to watch
the new mothers change

their babies' diapers,
the adolescent girls
and one albino boy
just outside the door

looking sweet enough
to forgive the inexplicable,
that none of us had come
to take them home.

Tug, tug all you like,
my darling—tug till you're back
asleep, tug in your dreams,
start tugging again

the minute you wake—
no matter how hard
you tug, your birthstone
necklace will not break.

Bear Claws

Lying on the chaise one morning with your daughter as she nurses
her bottle, her head resting in the crook of your arm, the two of you
looking out the French doors, gazing at the rosebed, the peonies,

the Siberian irises, your heart beating against her back, sounding out
her heart, you remember a friend drawing a bath in her cabin
one afternoon two summers before, dropping handfuls of seaweed

into the water, her daughter in the next room, reading on the floor
on her stomach. She read while you immured yourself in the water,
and everyone else, out hunting for chanterelles, got caught in rain.

When you close your eyes, you picture, involuntarily, how closing
your eyes in the bath it felt like a sea cave, water gently wafting
seaweed against your skin, but instead of small translucent fish,

swaying anemones, you kept seeing gash marks bear claws had made
in the aspen bark, and feeling the jolts of your friend's jeep careening
down the mountain, the slight sticky wetness of blood as it began

to pool on the saddle blanket covering your seat. You marvel
that your daughter, now flesh-and-blood, poking at your eyelid,
but then a mere idea to you, form after convoluted INS form,

had already so managed to take hold in your consciousness
that all summer you felt her vulnerability pressing in on the air,
and, melancholy, divided, sought to reassure her, to reassure

yourself, whispering, I want both of you, *I want you both.*
Now, kissing your daughter's forehead, lightly licking her cheek
to make her laugh, you see that even as your tears added salt

to the seaweed and your blood turned the bath water red, even as the sac slipped out, your daughter, your lotus bud, already was on her way, even as you wondered that bears could climb so high.

Anastylosis

Was it *my* wrist contused in the sarcophagic groove
under a bas-relief horse's red-stained hoof?

Again, at 2 A.M., a coyote's loopy truncated yelp,
a warbling unearthly and nervous as a car alarm.

If you hold me I have a chance to sleep.
But to unbox my thoughts, I need a hypnagogic.

*

In the backseat, one eye closed against the wind,
I nibbled sunflower seeds out of a paper cone

and tried to imagine the hillside zipping by
without condos, a day unclouded by moods.

At Troy you could still sense Helen, breathy
on the ruined rampart, pointing out each Greek

leader to Priam, familially whispering their names.
The bay was closer then, the battlefield

not half so wide a plain. No one had heard
of Schliemann, or—unimaginable—Homer.

At Avyalik, crook-necked satellite dishes
aproned every balcony like housebound wives

who bend over flower pots while straining
to catch an earful of gossip to transmit inside:

news of a nephew looking for work in Munich,
Pergamon's Great trapeziform Altar of Zeus

bartered off for transnational train tracks,
reconstructed, and housed since 1902 in Berlin.

The bitter smell of olive oil pooling in the sea air
fills our car. What was it I was thinking?

A tractor's parallel-parked on the main thoroughfare.
Limpid fingers worry the amber between her breasts.

*

There must be a name
for the marble columns'
cylindrical segments

collected and numbered
on the ruins' back lots
like a junkyard lot

of discarded tires
that still retain bite
on chiseled treads.

Isn't the life-span
of rubber almost as
long as marble's?

How long can a ruin
of excavated marble,
stone, last, patched

with ground marble,
white cement? Once,
I epoxied rancor to

extend the half-life
of love. In marble
we find the breakage,

the erosion, beautiful;
we *preserve* cracks,
swoon over Androklos'

smooth-muscled torso,
three and three-quarters
of its limbs hacked off.

*

Don't drink—in three languages—
from the sacred spring,
a pool of algae, stone catchment
in which, on a concrete pad,

fluorescent on khaki green,
wells up like an old definition
of *sconce*, a bilge-cloaked
bug-eyed frog the scum's crowned

to watch, under its dominion,
the once curative water
dribble in from a metal pipe,
squeeze out a weep hole.

Soaked up in a runnel
of the *cryptoportico's* caked throat,
stuck in the specific density,
mud, of its destiny, this water

sheds no runoff to wet the stones
of the Asklepion's now roofless
"communal incubation house"
where, nevertheless, I found

in a t-shaped crevice
of an archway's pier, cutaneous
evidence of the therapeutic arts,
a snakelet's translucent skin.

*

On the advice of Arlene Brill of Brill Bros. & Co.,
now defunct importers of garlic (two to a box),

we waited for the guard to shutter his ticket booth
before walking up to Athena's Temple, hidden

in the thickets above our *pansiyon*. By then the moon
had managed to vault the headlands of Lesbos

and the pocked marble gleamed under the polish of her gaze,
although, like us, she was only three-quarters there

and wobbly from *raki*. Cross-legged on the plinth
of a broken pedestal, I steadied myself and let myself

be lulled by the doubled lights of three night fishermen
following their brilliant-cut reflections home to what

I thought of as Sappho's own harbor across the bay.
The crickets were ubiquitous; unanimous, if noncommittal:

their stridulations as steady a backbeat to the music
drifting up from the beach hotel as they must have been

to Apollo's lyre. And if, in that heady atmosphere,
I ended up conflating Sappho, Aphrodite's darling,

with Athena, pledging the same unwritten stanzas
I labor on now to both—who overheard me?

Not the American couple strolling in as we left,
only one somnambulatory cow grazing the promontory.

*

If I use the word *oracle* do you think *person, place,* or *pronouncement?*

In a dream two octopi raised themselves out of a circle of orange eels and glided toward me.

Oracle can mean altar, priestess, or prophecy (marble, flesh, smoke).

While a reconstructed temple may give the impression of what it had been like unfragmented, anastylosis keeps the new materials, the repairs and cracks, visible,

as if to make us see, at the same time, the past out of one eye and the present out of the other (the future out of a third).

Centuries ago I might have told you "we visited Didyma . . . an oracle second only to Delphi . . . the oracle was mute . . . the oracle was dire."

When the octopi reached me, each coiled a tentacle around one of my wrists, squeezing so tightly I was certain this was the form my death would take—though I found that when I unclenched my fists the pressure eased.

Only later did you tell me that drum is the word for the cylinders.

*

We were barefoot. It was so hot
on the terrace the rag she wet
and wrung out for us to stand on
sizzled when she laid it down

but cooled our blistering feet.
A sea breeze shook the string
of goat bells on the garden gate
when, out of nowhere, I got stung

by a hovering swarm of tears.
It must be contemplating Lesbos
looming so close across the bay
that's made me lachrymose,

I lied, to avoid having to say
rag, and bucket on the stairs;
it was only that one gesture's
beauty brought me to tears.

*

At the end of the dream
I dreamt I wrote it down.

Thinking about the oracle,
a woman, as a conduit

inhabiting a sacred place,
the *oracle,* and receiving

from—from where?—
an *oracle,* the divination,

I started to wonder, was it
the vision or the visionary,

the *flesh* or the *smoke,*
that causes an oracle's

obliquity? When I woke
the knob of my left wrist

ached, but there were no
marks, no welt or bruises, no

notations: only coyote scat
studded with plum pits,

blue and slick from the skins,
smeared in the gravel

not four steps from our door,
and, like traces of pigment

staining a sarcophagus,
dawn's diaphanous scrawl.

Notes

1. The last line of "Studies in Pen and Ink" refers to a statement from Martin Luther: "Just because a bird flies over your head doesn't mean you have to build a nest for it in your hair."

2. In "Lou Reed in Istanbul," the lines *"swoop/swoop, oh baby, rock,/rock"* are from "Andy's Chest" on the 1972 album, *Transformer*.

3. The italicized lines in the second section of "Pelagos" are from George Seferis' *Collected Poems 1924-1975*, translated by Edmund Keeley and Phillip Sherrard (Jonathan Cape, 1973).

4. The Lightning Field is a site-specific installation by Walter De Maria, outside of Quemado, New Mexico, open to visitors by appointment. The factual statements about the field in sections 1, 3, and 16 of the poem are taken from the artist's statement, entitled "Some Facts, Notes, Data, Information, Statistics, and Statements," which can be found in *Artforum*, XVIII: 8 (April 1980). A pseudomorph (section 12) is a piece of silk whose physical structure survives imprinted on the patina of ancient bronze vessels.